The
EVEN
BIGGER
BOOK OF
GROSS
JOKES

The
EVEN
BIGGER
BOOK OF
GROSS
JOKES

• • • •

Julius Alvin

𝒦

KENSINGTON BOOKS
http://www.kensingtonbooks.com

KENSINGTON BOOKS are published by
Kensington Publishing Corp.
850 Third Avenue
New York, NY 10022

All Kensington titles, imprints and distributed lines are available at special quantity discounts for bulk purchases for sales promotion, premiums, fund raising, educational or institutional use.

Special book excerpts or customized printings can also be created to fit specific needs. For details, write or phone the office of the Kensington Special Sales Manager: Kensington Publishing Corp., 850 Third Avenue, New York, NY, Attn. Special Sales Department. Phone: 1-800-221-2647.

Kensington and the K logo Reg. U.S. Pat. & TM Off.

ISBN 1-57566-789-4

First Printing: December, 2000
10 9 8 7 6 5 4 3 2

Printed in the United States of America

CONTENTS

A
TRULY
GROSS
VARIETY

● ● ● ● ● ● ●

A Polish woman went to the drugstore and asked the clerk to sell her some deodorant for her husband.

"Certainly, madam," answered the clerk, "would that be the ball type?"

The Polish woman replied, "Oh, no. It's for under his arms."

• • •

A surgeon came to see his patient on the morning after her operation. The young blonde asked him, somewhat hesitantly, how long it would be before she could resume her normally active sex life.

"I really haven't thought about it," said the surgeon. "You're the first patient who's ever asked me that question after a tonsillectomy!"

• • •

What's small, red, and spins round at 2000 rpm?

A baby picking its nose with a power drill.

• • •

What did the black kid get for his birthday?

My bicycle.

• • •

Why can't black guys do pushups?

Because their lips stick them to the floor on the first "down."

• • •

Did you hear about the leper prostitute who had to quit her job?

Her business fell off.

• • •

Why is a laundromat a bad place for a guy to pick up women?

Because any woman who can't even afford a washing machine will never be able to support you.

• • •

What do you call a dyslexic genius?

Brians.

• • •

5

How did Kurt Cobain collect his final thoughts?

With a spatula.

. . .

What is a surefire sign that the girl you just met is a Jewish American Princess?

She thinks that "cooking" and "fucking" are two cities in China.

. . .

How can you tell if you're at a Scotsman's stag party?

When a sheep jumps out of the cake.

. . .

Did you hear about the one-legged girl who got raped?

She couldn't cross her legs to save her ass.

• • •

What is another name for a Scotsman with lots of girlfriends?

Shepherd.

• • •

How can a woman make a man eat shit?

Marry him.

• • •

What should you do if an epileptic has a fit in your bathtub?

Throw in your dirty laundry and some soap.

• • •

What was Christa McAuliff doing on the Space Shuttle in the first place?

They figured out she was 65 pounds lighter than a regular dishwasher.

• • •

Did you hear about the new record label specializing in gangsta rap?

It's called "Mowdown."

• • •

What does a woman have in common with a Kentucky Fried Chicken?

When you're finished with the thigh and breast, you've still got a greasy box to stick your bone in.

• • •

How can you tell if a leper has been using your shower?

Your bar of soap has gotten bigger.

• • •

Two bums were thirsty, but only had fifty cents between them. The first bum came up with an idea, took the fifty cents, and bought a hot dog.

"What is that going to get us to drink?" asked the second bum.

"I'll show you," says the first one. "Just stuff the hot dog down the front of your pants and follow me."

The two went to the nearest bar where they each ordered a double whiskey. As the bartender approached them with the bill, the first bum promptly leaned over into his pal's lap, unzipped his fly, then pulled out the hot dog and started sucking on it.

"How gross!" shouted the bartender. "Two fags doing it right here in public! Get out of my bar this instant!"

Their plan worked equally as well at the next bar, the next, and so on for eight more stops. Finally, with their alcoholic needs fully satisfied, they stumbled back to the alley they called home.

"Well, see how much pleasure we got out of one plain old hot dog?" the first bum said.

"You don't know the half of it," the second bum replied. "I lost the hot dog after the second bar!"

• • •

What do you call a woman with a toothpick through her clit?

Olive.

• • •

Why can't girls wear miniskirts in the winter?

Chapped lips.

• • •

How can you tell when your chick is too fat to fuck?

When you pull her panties down to her knees, and her pussy is still in them.

• • •

What is the only good thing about Women's Lib?

It gives them something to do with all their spare time.

• • •

TEN THINGS NOT TO SAY TO A COP WHEN YOU GET STOPPED

1. I can't reach my license unless you hold my beer.

2. Sorry, Officer, I didn't realize my radar detector wasn't plugged in.

3. Aren't you the guy from the Village People?

4. Hey, you must've been doin' about 125 mph to keep up with me! Good job!

5. Excuse me. Is "stick 'em up" hyphenated?

6. I thought you had to be in relatively good physical condition to be a police officer.

7. I was going to be a cop, but I decided to finish high school instead.

8. You're not gonna check the trunk, are you?

9. Is it true that people become cops because they are too dumb to work at McDonald's?

10. Well, when I reached down to pick up my bag of crack, my gun fell off my lap and got lodged between the brake pedal and the gas pedal, forcing me to speed out of control.

• • •

How is an old lady like Australia?

Everyone knows what's "down under" but who gives a shit?

• • •

How is getting head from Hillary Clinton like walking a tightrope across the Grand Canyon?

In neither case do you want to look down.

• • •

What is a 72?

69 with a 5 percent meal tax.

• • •

Did you hear about the blonde whose boyfriend told her he loved her?

She believed him.

• • •

How can you tell if your ladder was manufactured in Poland?

There is a sign on the top step that says, "stop."

• • •

A black guy walks up to a Southerner, who's playing with his pet raccoon.

Never having seen such an animal before the black guy asks the redneck, "Hey, what kind of critter be dat?"

"It's the same as what y'all been called all your life," the redneck replies.

"No shit?" the black guy asks. "It's called a motherfucker?"

• • •

Name the two things that went off in Andrew Cunanan's mouth.

A Colt .44 and Gianni Versace.

• • •

Why did the Jew cross the road?

To franchise the other side.

• • •

What's the best thing Kurt Cobain ever released?

The safety.

• • •

How do you get a man to do situps?

Glue the TV remote between his ankles.

• • •

What do a dog and a gynecologist have in common?

They both have wet noses.

• • •

Why did Karen Carpenter finally have to shoot her dog?

Because he kept trying to bury her.

• • •

What is the difference between a Polish woman and a Bigfoot?

One is six feet tall, dirty, hairy, and smelly, and the other just has really big feet.

• • •

A man was screwing an old whore and she asked him, "Say, that ring you are wearing is a little uncomfortable, do you mind taking it off?"
    He said to her, "That's not my ring, that's my watch!"

• • •

What's the difference between Hillary and Rock Hudson?

Hillary's aides haven't killed her yet.

• • •

Did you hear about the new jeans Calvin Klein designed for faggots?

They have kneepads in front and a zippered trapdoor on the ass.

• • •

What's the difference between a lawyer and a vulture?

When the lawyer goes to sleep, he takes off his wingtips.

• • •

A priest, a rabbi, and a minister were enjoying beers together at the local tavern. Suddenly a fly landed in the priest's beer. The priest gently scooped the fly out, released it, and exclaimed, "Fly away free, you little creature of God!"

After a couple of minutes, the fly returned and landed in the minister's beer. Not to be outdone in demonstration of his faith, the minister scooped the fly out carefully and released it, saying, "Fly away free, you little creature of God!"

Not more than five minutes passed when the fly returned and made a nosedive into the rabbi's beer. He responded by grabbing it back out and pulling its wings as he shouted, "Spit my beer back in the glass, you alcoholic son-of-a-bitch!"

• • •

So this housewife got a phone call from the brewery where her husband worked. The foreman told her, "I'm sorry to inform you, ma'am, that your husband drowned today in one of our vats of beer."

"Oh, my God! Was it quick?" the wife asks.

"No, it took some time," the foreman said.

"Well, then, did he suffer much?"

"I don't think so," was the reply. "He got out on four separate occasions to urinate before he went under for the final time."

● ● ●

What's more cruel than sending an anniversary card to Yoko Ono?

Sending a Father's Day card to JonBenet Ramsey's father.

● ● ●

What is grosser than gross?

When you wake up in a strange bed one morning and find a lump in your throat, then realize that there's a string attached to it.

• • •

Why did it take the Polish couple six weeks to drive across the U.S.?

Because they kept encountering signs that said, "Clean Rest Rooms."

• • •

How did the Polish woman keep her son from biting his nails?

She made him wear shoes.

• • •

What's the definition of "necrophilia?"

The urge to pop a cold one.

• • •

How do Polish girls protect themselves from peep-ing toms?

They leave their curtains open.

• • •

What is the Alzheimer's society slogan?

"Remember those who can't."

• • •

SIGNS YOU SHOULD BREAK UP WITH
YOUR BOYFRIEND

1. He always scratches his crotch and says, "Damn! "When is this gonna clear up?"
2. He could use a contact lens as a condom.
3. Taking you out to eat means firing up the grill.
4. Every time you want to spoon, he wants to fork.
5. He refers to your little brother as a "real cutie."

SIGNS YOU SHOULD BREAK UP WITH
YOUR GIRLFRIEND

1. She carries around *Bride* magazine and a highlighter.
2. She thinks an anniversary occurs once a month.
3. Her lucky numbers are your pin number.
4. Your friends know her by her porn name.
5. She just can't stand the taste of "it."

• • •

Why do women have babies?

Because it hurts and they deserve it.

• • •

Why can't Italian men give their wives mink coats?

Because the fur clashes with their wives' moustaches.

• • •

How do Eskimos give birth?

They start out by rubbing noses, and pretty soon the little buggers fall out.

• • •

How do you make Italian sausage?

From retarded pigs.

• • •

How many chiropractors does it take to change a lightbulb?

One, but it takes twenty visits.

• • •

What is the one social advantage to being Polish?

You never miss a phone call due to being in the bathtub.

• • •

Why is it traditional to boil water when a woman is giving birth to a baby?

Because if the baby dies, you can make soup.

• • •

A Polish woman went to see her doctor because of serious abrasions on her knees.

"Do you know what caused these injuries?" the doctor asked.

"Well," she replied, "I've been having sex doggie style."

"Oh, that's no problem," the doctor said. "Just roll over and do it missionary style for awhile."

"Oh, but that is a problem," the Polish woman said. "Every time I try it that way, my dog's breath makes me puke!"

• • •

What do you do when your cat spits at you?

Turn the grill down.

• • •

Why did the little girl keep a dead goldfish in her pocket?

Because she wanted to smell just like a big girl.

• • •

A Polack was dragged in for a blood test during a paternity suit. He went into the doctor's office terribly nervous, but came out smiling and confident.

"Why you so happy?" his friend asked.

"I have nothing to worry about now," the Polack said. "That stupid doctor took the blood sample from my finger!"

• • •

A Truly Gross Variety

Why don't blondes in San Francisco wear short miniskirts?

Because their balls show!

• • •

What was Mickey Mantle's favorite part of a baseball game?

The bottom of the fifth.

• • •

A man came home from a poker game late one night and found his bitchy, nagging wife waiting for him with a rolling pin.

"Where the hell have you been?" she asked.

"You'll have to pack all your things, dear," he said. "I've just lost you in a card game."

"How did you manage to do that?" she wanted to know.

"It wasn't easy," the husband said. "I had to fold with four aces."

• • •

Two gay guys are in a hot tub pushing a big turd back and forth in the water. Another guy walks by and asks, "What the hell are you two doing?"

The first fag replies, "We're teaching our baby how to swim!"

• • •

What's the definition of "tragedy?"

When your girlfriend puts her bra on backwards, and it fits.

• • •

Two women were in the waiting room of an abortion clinic, when one noticed that the other was knitting what looked like a tiny, blue baby bonnet.

The first lady said to the knitter, "Excuse me, but don't you regard it as at least mildly tasteless to be sewing a baby bonnet when you are about to have an abortion?"

"No," the second lady said. "You see, it's not a baby bonnet, it's a body bag."

• • •

A middle-aged woman took a taxi home, but when they arrived at their destination, she discovered that she had no money. She lifted up her dress, dropped her panties and shouted to the cabbie, "How's about taking out what I owe you in trade?"

The cabbie looked and said, "Lady, don't you have anything smaller?"

• • •

Why do they play sports on artificial turf in Poland?

To keep the cheerleaders from grazing.

• • •

Why did the feminist commit suicide?

She saw herself in the mirror.

• • •

Why don't vampires go south of the border?

Because every time they suck a Mexican's blood, they get the shits for a month.

• • •

What's the definition of a "fart?"

A Greek love call.

• • •

How are women like condoms?

When they're not hanging off the end of your dick, they're in your wallet.

• • •

How do you tell if an Arkansas girl is old enough to marry?

Make her stand in a barrel. If her chin is over the top, she's old enough. If it isn't, cut the barrel down a bit.

• • •

What do you call a prostitute with a runny nose?

Full.

• • •

Why do Southern guys go to family reunions?

To meet chicks.

• • •

What is the difference between tampons and mobile phones?

Mobile phones are for assholes.

• • •

What did Jeffrey Dahmer say to Pee Wee Herman in their holding cell at the jail?

"Stop playing with my lunch."

• • •

How do you get a horny dog to stop humping on your leg?

Pick him up and start sucking his dick.

• • •

Why does a bride smile when she walks up the aisle?

She knows she's given her last blowjob.

• • •

There's a new sitcom out directed especially at gay men.

It's called, *Leave It, It's Beaver.*

• • •

How do you know a blonde has just lost her virginity?

Her crayons are still sticky.

• • •

What do pussy and a warm toilet seat have in common?

They're both nice but you always wonder about who was there before you.

• • •

Why did the husband stop having anal sex with his wife?

Because every night it was the same old shit.

• • •

How can you tell when an auto mechanic just had sex?

One of his fingers is clean.

• • •

A Truly Gross Variety

What's brown and smells nice?

A big turd in a bubble bath.

• • •

How does a Puerto Rican get into an honest business?

Through the skylight.

• • •

What's green and melts in your mouth?

A leper's dick.

• • •

What's twenty feet long and smells like piss?

The conga line at an old-age home.

• • •

How do people in Alabama practice safe sex?

They spray paint X's on the back of the animals that kick.

• • •

Why did the pervert cross the road?

Because he had his dick stuck up the chicken's ass.

• • •

What is the difference between a battery and a woman?

A battery has a positive side.

• • •

What's the difference between Christopher Reeve and O.J. Simpson?

Christopher Reeve got the electric chair and O.J. walked!

• • •

How many men does it take to open a beer?

None. It should be open by the time the bitch brings it.

• • •

Why doesn't Smokey the Bear have any children?

Because whenever his wife gets hot he beats her with a shovel.

• • •

Why do the men in Scotland wear kilts?

Because the sheep can hear a zipper a mile away.

• • •

What did God say when he saw Eve swimming in the ocean?

"Shit—it's gonna take me millions of years to get that smell outta those fish!"

• • •

What do you call eight days of blowjobs?

Hanukkah Lewinsky.

• • •

What do you call twenty bulldykes with assault rifles?

Militia Etheridge.

• • •

Why do gay men wear ribbed condoms?

They get better traction in the mud.

• • •

What do you call a bouncer at a gay bar?

A flame thrower.

. . .

Why do so many women fake orgasm?

Because so many men fake foreplay.

. . .

What's the best part of eating cherry pie yet the worst part of eating hair pie?

The crust.

. . .

What's white and clings to a toilet wall?

George Michael's latest release.

. . .

What's the definition of "trust?"

Two cannibals giving each other a blowjob.

• • •

What's the definition of African-American aristocracy?

A man who can trace his lineage back to his father.

• • •

How can you tell if your husband is dead?

The sex is the same, but you get the remote.

• • •

What's the difference between menstrual blood and sand?

You can't gargle with sand.

• • •

What do vegetarian worms eat?

Linda McCartney.

• • •

What happens when you take Viagra with Valium?

If you don't get a fuck you don't give a fuck.

• • •

How do you get a man to eat shit?

Wipe forwards.

• • •

Why do men find it difficult to make eye contact?

Because tits don't have eyes.

• • •

Why are hangovers better than women?

Because hangovers will go away.

• • •

What's the difference between a good ol' boy and a redneck?

The good ol' boy raises livestock. The redneck gets emotionally involved.

• • •

How can you tell if a redneck is married?

There are tobacco spit stains on both sides of his pickup truck.

• • •

Why isn't George Michael allowed to vote?

He can't go into a cubicle alone.

• • •

The husband says, "Let's try a different position tonight."

The wife replies, "Okay—you stand by the ironing board while I sit on the sofa and fart."

• • •

Two cannibal chiefs sit licking their fingers after a large meal. "Your wife makes a delicious roast," one chief says.

"Thanks," his friend says. "I'm gonna miss her."

• • •

What do Disney World and Viagra have in common?

They both make you wait an hour for a two-minute ride.

• • •

What's the difference between a Ritz and a lesbian?

One's a snack cracker, the other's a crack snacker.

• • •

What's the most popular pick-up line in Alabama?

"Nice tooth!"

• • •

Why is a pap smear called a pap smear?

Because women wouldn't have them if they were called cunt scrapes.

• • •

What does Hillary Clinton do right after she shaves her pussy?

She sends him to work.

• • •

Why don't women blink during foreplay?

They don't have time.

• • •

What do you call a truck driver with a load of sheep headed for Montana?

A pimp.

• • •

What's brown and often found in children's under-pants?

Michael Jackson's hand.

• • •

What do you call a guy from Arkansas who doesn't fuck his sister?

An only child.

• • •

What do women and shrimp have in common?

Their heads are full of shit, but the pink part tastes nice.

• • •

Why do men take showers instead of baths?

Because pissing in the bath is disgusting.

• • •

What's the difference between a doberman and a social worker?

You get your baby back from a doberman.

• • •

What's the difference between acne and a priest?

Acne usually comes on a boy's face AFTER he turns thirteen.

• • •

Why do tampons have strings?

So you can floss after eating.

• • •

What's the difference between driving in the fog and eating pussy?

It's that when you eat pussy, you can see the asshole in front of you.

• • •

What do you call five dogs with no balls?

The Spice Girls.

• • •

What do Chris Farley and Michael Kennedy have in common?

They both died on white powder.

• • •

How many women does it take to paint a wall?

Depends on how hard you throw them.

• • •

What's the difference between a lawyer and a trampoline?

You take off your shoes to jump on a trampoline!

• • •

Why does Mike Tyson cry during sex?

Mace.

• • •

What is the difference between Prince Charles and O.J. Simpson?

Prince Charles's ex-wife was killed by a white man in a black car.

• • •

What do you call a vegetarian with diarrhea?

A salad shooter.

• • •

What does it mean when your wife keeps coming out of the kitchen to nag you?

You made her chain too long.

• • •

What has four legs and eight arms?

A pit-bull terrier in a playground.

• • •

How do men sort their laundry?

Filthy and *Filthy but wearable.*

• • •

Why do women have arms?

Because it takes too long to lick the bathroom clean.

• • •

A Truly Gross Variety

How do you know you're a real loser?

A nymphomaniac tells you, "Let's just be friends."

• • •

What has a whole bunch of little balls and screws old ladies?

A bingo machine.

• • •

One cannibal says to the other, "Who was that lady I saw you with last night?"

The second cannibal says, "That was no lady, that was my lunch."

• • •

THE REAL MEANING BEHIND THE ABBREVIATIONS IN PERSONAL ADS.

FIRST THE WOMEN:

40-ish	48
Adventurer	Has had more partners than you ever will
Athletic	Flat-chested
Average looking	Ugly
Beautiful	Pathological liar
Contagious smile	Bring your penicillin
Educated	College dropout
Emotionally secure	Medicated
Free spirit	Substance user
Friendship first	Trying to live down reputation as slut
Fun	Annoying
Gentle	Comatose
Good listener	Borderline autistic
New-Age	All body hair, all the time
Old-fashioned	Lights out, missionary position only
Open-minded	Desperate
Outgoing	Loud
Passionate	Loud
Poet	Depressive schizophrenic
Professional	Real witch
Redhead	Shops the Clairol section
Reubenesque	Grossly fat
Romantic	Looks better by candlelight
Voluptuous	Very fat

Wants soulmate	One step away from stalking
Widow	Nagged first husband to death
Young at heart	Toothless crone

THE MALE SIDE OF THE LIST:

40-ish	52 and looking for 25-year-old
Athletic	Sits on the couch and watches ESPN
Average looking	Unusual hair growth on ears, nose, and back
Educated	Will always treat you like an idiot
Free spirit	Sleeps with your sister
Friendship first	As long as friendship involves nudity
Fun	Good with a remote and a six-pack
Good looking	Arrogant
Honest	Pathological liar
Huggable	Overweight, more body hair than a bear
Like to cuddle	Insecure, overly dependent
Mature	Until you get to know him
Open-minded	Wants to sleep with your sister but she's not interested

• • •

The two friends ran into each other on the streets of New York's garment district.

The first friend says, "I'm so sorry about the fire you had in your shop yesterday, is there anything I can do?"

The second one replies, "For God's sake shut up. The fire isn't until *tomorrow*."

• • •

The President and Hillary Clinton are in the front row at a Yankees game. The row behind them is taken up with Secret Service agents. One of them leans over and whispers in the President's ear. Mr. Clinton pauses, then grabs Hillary by the scruff of the neck and heaves her over the railing. She falls ten feet to the top of the dugout, kicking and screaming obscenities.

The Secret Service agent leans over again and whispers, "Mr. President, I said they want you to throw out the first PITCH!"

• • •

A redneck has sex with his sister. Afterwards, she says, "You fuck a lot better than Daddy does."

Her brother replies, "I should—Mommy taught me everything I know."

• • •

It's the day after Christmas and two kids are comparing notes about what they'd gotten. The first kid says, "What'd you get?"

The second kid replies, "Man, I made out! I got Power Rangers stuff, Nintendo, a new bike, a Walkie-Talkie set, a stereo, and a whole lot more! What'd you get?"

"Ah, I just got a baseball glove and bat," says the first kid.

"Wow, that's pretty rough," says the second kid.

The first kid says, "Yeah, well, at least I'm not dying of cancer."

• • •

A man calls into work sick and says to his boss, "I can't come in today. I'm really sick. I've been in bed all day."

The boss says, "Are you crazy? This is the day we are meeting with our most important account!"

The man replies, "I'm really sorry boss, but I'm *really* sick."

The boss asks, "Just how sick can one man be?"

"Well for starters," the man says, "right now I'm fucking my five-year-old daughter."

• • •

A fag wakes in the morning and walks into the kitchen, and sees his boyfriend jacking off into a bag.

The first gay guy asks his boyfriend, "What are you doing?"

"What do you think I'm doing?" his boyfriend replies. "I'm packing your lunch."

• • •

A man is in the shower with his six-year-old daughter when she asks "What's that between your legs, Daddy?"

"That's a penis, honey," he replies.

"Will I ever get one?" she asks.

"Yes," Daddy answers. "Just as soon as Mommy leaves for work."

• • •

A man is desperate for sex. He goes to a whorehouse with only five dollars to his name. He approaches the madam of the house who politely informs him that five dollars won't get him anything. He pleads and pleads for sex until the madam finally tells him, "OK, go to room five."

Our horny dude heads over to room five, opens the door and sees this just absolutely beautiful blond girl lying there naked. Without any hesitation, he jumps on her and starts going at it. Five hours later, he's almost done when sperm starts coming out of her ears, her eyes, her mouth . . . everywhere! The guy freaks and runs to tell the madam what happened.

"Someone get in here with a mop," she yells out. "The dead girl in room five is full again!"

• • •

Why can't Ray Charles read?

Because he's black.

• • •

What is purple with pink polka dots and sits on my porch?

My nigger, and I'll paint him whatever colors I want!

• • •

What's the worst thing about eating bald pussy?

The diaper.

• • •

A man walks into a bar and sits down at a table. He notices a leper at the bar.

The man orders a shot, drinks the shot and then throws up. Next he orders a beer, drinks the beer and then throws up. He does this for several more drinks when finally the leper comes over to his table and tells him, "I'm sorry if my appearance is making you sick."

The man replies, "No, it's not you. It's the man next to you dipping his potato chips into your neck."

• • •

What would they have called the Flintstones if they were black?

Fucking niggers.

• • •

A little girl is playing by the side of the road when a man pulls up in a car. The man leans out and says, "Hey little girl, would you like some candy?"

The girl looks over and says, "My mommy told me not to take candy from strangers . . . but if you give me twenty dollars, I'll suck your dick."

• • •

What's the worst thing about eating vegetables?

Putting them back in the wheelchair when you're done.

• • •

What's the worst thing about screwing a five-year-old girl?

Hearing she's had better.

• • •

A black guy walks into a bar, sits down and says to the white guy next to him, "I'm blacker than hell, I've got a pecker named Mel, and I just love fucking white women."

Frightened, the white guy takes off.

The black guy, feeling quite good about himself turns to another white guy and says, "I'm blacker than hell, I've got a pecker named Mel, and I just love fucking white women."

The second white guy takes off, too.

Smiling to himself, the black guy spots his next victim, turns to him and says, "I'm blacker than hell, I've got a pecker named Mel, and I just love fucking white women."

The third guy says, "I don't blame you. I wouldn't fuck a nigger either!"

• • •

What's warm, bloody and crawls up your leg?

A homesick abortion.

• • •

What do you tell a woman with two black eyes?

Nothing—you already told her twice.

• • •

What's the first thing a woman does when she gets out of the battered women's shelter?

The dishes, if she knows what's good for her.

• • •

What's the best thing God ever did?

He invented pussy.

• • •

What's the worst thing He ever did?

He put women in charge of it.

• • •

Why did the woman cross the road?

Because I told her to.

• • •

What does every feminist in this world need?

A good man to smack some sense into her.

• • •

Why can't men get mad cow disease?

Because they're pigs.

• • •

What do you call a man with 99% of his brain missing?

Castrated.

• • •

Why are men like chocolate bars?

They're sweet, smooth, and they usually head right for your hips.

• • •

A little boy was taking a shower with his mother when he looked between her legs and asked, "Mommy, what's that?"

"Well honey," she replied, "that's where God touched me with His golden axe."

The little boy said, "He smacked you in the cunt with a golden axe? Didn't that hurt?"

• • •

What did the gay guy say to his boyfriend when they passed the funeral parlor?

"Let's go inside and suck down a couple cold ones."

• • •

A guy walks into a bar down in Alabama and orders milk. Surprised, the bartender looks around and says, "You ain't from around here . . . where you from, boy?"

The guy says, "I'm from Pennsylvania."

The bartender asks, "What do you do up in Pennsylvania?"

The guy responds, "I'm a taxidermist."

The bartender asks, "A taxidermist . . . what the hell is a taxidermist?"

The guy says, "I mount dead animals."

The bartender smiles and shouts to the whole bar, "It's okay, boys, he's one of us!"

• • •

What's worse than jock itch?

Four blondes at a 4-way stop sign.

• • •

A man walks into a bar and asks for six shots of vodka. The bartender says, "Six shots? What's wrong?"

"I found out my older brother is gay," the man says.

The next night, he walks into the bar again and asks for six shots of vodka.

"What now?" asked the bartender.

"I found out my younger brother is gay," replied the man.

The night after that, the man walked into the bar again and asked for six shots of vodka.

"Shit," the bartender says. "Does anybody in your family like women?"

The man replies, "Yeah, my wife."

• • •

GROSS ETHNIC JOKES AND MORE

● ● ● ● ● ● ●

What is a black birth certificate?

A refund letter from a condom company.

• • •

What do you call a tampon used by Nazis?

A Twatstika.

• • •

What is the worst foursome in golf? O.J. Simpson, Heidi Fleiss, Ted Kennedy and Greg Louganis.

Why are they the worst? Well, O.J. slices . . . Fleiss hooks . . . Kennedy drives everything into the water, and Louganis doesn't know which hole to put it in!

• • •

How did Miss Puerto Rico win the talent competition at the Miss America contest?

She stripped a Cadillac in three minutes flat.

• • •

Why haven't any women astronauts ever been sent to the Moon?

Because the moon doesn't need cleaning.

• • •

How can you tell who is the Irish guy in the hospital?

He's the one blowing the foam off of his bedpan.

• • •

What's the difference between a lawyer and a vampire?

A vampire only sucks blood at night.

• • •

How can you tell if an Italian woman is embarrassed by her long, black hair?

She wears long, black gloves to cover it up.

• • •

What type of cards do they accept at Korean restaurants?

Blue Cross and Blue Shield.

• • •

What caused the birth rate in Poland to skyrocket?

When they started giving paper bags out to customers at grocery stores.

• • •

What do you call a fight between two Chinese lesbians?

A tong war.

• • •

A Frenchman and an Italian were seated next to a Texan on an overseas flight. After a few cocktails, the men began discussing their home lives.

"Last night I made love to my wife four times," the Frenchman bragged, "and this morning she made me delicious crepes and she told me how much she adored me."

"Ah, last night I made love to my wife six times," the Italian responded, "and this morning she made me a wonderful omelet and told me she could never love another man."

When the Texan remained silent, the Frenchman smugly asked, "And how many times did you make love to your wife last night?"

"Once," he replied.

"Only once?" the Italian asked. "And what did she say to you this morning?"

The Texan replied, "Don't stop."

• • •

How do you turn a triangle into a straight line?

Shave it.

• • •

How can you tell if a girl is a genuine redneck?

When she can suck a dick and chew tobacco at the same time, and know what to spit and what to swallow.

• • •

What is an Italian's concept of a "10?"

No moustache.

• • •

Why don't Arabs get circumcised?

So they'll have some place to park their gum during sandstorms.

• • •

How does a Puerto Rican social event review in the paper always begin?

"Among those wounded in the gunfire were . . ."

• • •

What do you say to a Puerto Rican business executive?

"I'll take a dime bag."

• • •

Did you hear they came out with a new Oprah doll?

Ken and Barbie needed a maid.

• • •

Why should you be suspicious of any guy who keeps passing gas around you?

Because farts are faggots' mating calls.

• • •

What do Clinton and JFK have in common?

Both of their careers ended with a stained dress.

• • •

What do you do after you just raped a twelve-year-old deaf and dumb girl?

Break her fingers so she can't tell her mother.

• • •

After his annual physical, the sexually active bachelor was waiting in the doctor's office for the results.

"Well," said the doctor, "I have good news and bad news for you."

"The way I feel, please give me the good news first," replied the bachelor.

"The good news," announced the doctor, "is that your penis has grown an additional four inches since your last examination."

"Great!" the man shouted. "What is the bad news?"

"It's malignant," replied the doctor.

• • •

What does a lesbian do when her secretary makes a mistake?

Gives her a good tongue-lashing.

• • •

What's the worst part about getting a lung transplant?

The first couple of times you cough, it's not your phlegm.

• • •

Why do pedophiles like Halloween?

Free home delivery.

• • •

What is a shit?

A queer's wet dream.

• • •

What do you give the pedophile who has everything?

Another parish.

• • •

Why don't lawyers play hide-and-seek?

Nobody will look for them.

• • •

A woman gets on a bus, as she passes the driver he grabs his throat and makes choking noises. The woman starts crying and hits the driver with her purse. A few minutes later the buzzer goes off and the lady passes the driver as she is getting off the bus. The driver again grabs his throat and makes choking noises. The lady starts crying and again hits the driver with her purse.

A passenger sitting behind the driver asked him, "What is that all about?"

The driver replies, "Oh, her daughter hanged herself last night and I'm just teasing her."

• • •

How can you tell if a household is homosexual?

The welcome mat reads: "Please wipe your knees."

• • •

What is "love?"

The delusion that one woman is different from another.

• • •

How can a girl tell when she is really ugly?

When she has to have tits grafted onto her back just to get laid.

• • •

On a flight from New York to Miami, a man is surprised to see a parrot strapped in next to him. He asks the stewardess for coffee, whereupon the parrot squawks, "And get me a whiskey, you cow!"

The stewardess, flustered, brings back a whiskey for the parrot and forgets the coffee. The man asks for coffee a second time, and the parrot cries out to the stewardess, "And get me another whiskey, you bitch!"

The stewardess, really upset, comes back shaking with another whiskey but still no coffee. Getting angry, the man tries the parrot's approach, saying to the stewardess, "I've asked you twice for a coffee, go and get it now or I'll slap you silly."

The next moment both he and the parrot have been yanked out of their seats and thrown out of the emergency exit by the co-pilot and the navigator.

Plunging downward the parrot turns to the man and says, "You know, for someone who can't fly, you're a cheeky bastard!"

• • •

How can a girl tell when she is too flat-chested?

She applies for a job as a topless waitress and gets hired as a busboy.

• • •

What's better than winning a Gold Medal at the Special Olympics?

Not being a retard.

• • •

WHAT ARE TEN THINGS A MAN NEVER WANTS
TO HEAR WHEN HE'S NAKED?

1. I've smoked joints fatter than that.
2. Why don't we just cuddle?
3. My last boyfriend was four inches bigger.
4. My baby brother has one like yours.
5. Don't they have surgery to fix that?
6. Why is God punishing you?
7. Are you cold?
8. Why don't we skip right to the cigarettes?
9. It still works, right?
10. Awww—it's hiding!

• • •

How can you tell the Polack at an orgy?

He's the one who shows up with an artificial vagina as his date.

• • •

What happened to the Polack the first time he counted to twenty-one?

He got arrested for indecent exposure.

• • •

How can a girl tell if the guy trying to pick her up is a real loser?

He sends a glass of water over to her table.

• • •

What's the definition of a perfect blind date?

She comes to the door naked, carrying a sixpack.

• • •

What do you get if you cross a prostitute with an elephant?

A whore who does it for peanuts and remembers you forever.

• • •

THINGS NOT TO SAY TO A WOMAN DURING SEX

1. Did I tell you my Aunt Martha died in this bed?
2. On second thought, let's turn off the lights.
3. You're good enough to do this for a living.
4. Have you ever considered liposuction?
5. And to think, I didn't even have to buy you dinner!
6. I was so horny tonight, I would have taken anything home.
7. Keep it down, my mother is a light sleeper.
8. When is it going to be my friend's turn?
9. It's nice being in bed with something you don't have to inflate.
10. And to think, I was trying to pick up your friend!

• • •

How is a female like a toilet seat?

Without the hole in the middle, neither one would be good for shit.

• • •

Why do Italian men have moustaches?

So they can look like their mothers.

• • •

How is a clitoris like the state of North Dakota?

Most men know they're there, but few care.

• • •

Did you hear about the guy who got his vasectomy at Sears?

Every time he gets a hard-on, his garage door opens.

• • •

Why do blondes wear black panties?

To mourn the stiff they buried there the night before.

• • •

The young cannibal girl watched as her tribe lowered a missionary into their boiling cauldron.

"Now watch what happens next, dear," her mother instructed. "It is always easiest when we are cooking a man for dinner."

"Why is that?" asked her daughter.

"Because all you have to do to cook him precisely right is wait until his balls explode, then just add the potatoes and vegetables."

• • •

Why did the Polish athlete get thrown off the Olympic team?

They found traces of Pepsi in his blood.

• • •

What's barren, burned, and glows in the dark?

Iraq, if Clinton really had any balls.

• • •

What do Lucille Ball and Monica Lewinsky have in common?

They each had sex with a Cuban.

• • •

A young girl was having a heart-to-heart talk with her mother on her first visit home since starting university.

"Mom, I have to tell you," the girl confessed. "I lost my virginity last weekend."

"I'm not surprised," said her mother. "It was bound to happen sooner or later. I just hope it was a romantic and pleasurable experience."

"Well, yes and no," the girl replied. "The first eight guys felt great, but after them my cunt got really sore."

• • •

What do you get when you cross a Communist with a lesbian?

Chelsea Clinton.

• • •

FIVE THINGS NOT TO SAY TO YOUR PREGNANT WIFE

1. "How come you're so much fatter than the other chicks in Lamaze?"
2. "Hey, when you're finished pukin' in there, get me a beer, willya?"
3. "Yo, Fatass! You're blocking the TV!"
4. "Y'know, looking at her, you'd never guess that Pamela Lee had a baby!"
5. "I sure hope your thighs aren't gonna stay that flabby forever!"

• • •

How can you tell if you are in a gay amusement park?

They hand out gerbils at the tunnel of love.

• • •

What's the best thing about getting a blowjob from an Ethiopian chick?

You know she'll swallow.

• • •

What would happen if the earth spun thirty times faster than it does now?

Every day would be payday and all the women in the world would bleed to death.

• • •

Why do they put cotton in the tops of medicine bottles?

To remind black drug dealers that they were once slaves.

• • •

If an athlete gets athlete's foot, what does a gynecologist get?

Tunnel vision.

• • •

What's the best thing about being a pedophile?

Your dick looks really BIG in a little hand.

• • •

A black guy and a white guy are jogging side by side when they enter a tunnel. Which guy comes out of the tunnel first?

The white guy, because the black guy has to stop to write "motherfucker" on the wall.

• • •

Why did God create men?

Because vibrators can't take out the trash.

• • •

What's the definition of a sensitive guy?

Someone who doesn't make his girlfriend blow him after he buttfucks her.

• • •

How does a typical Teamster tell bedtime fairy tales to his kids?

"Once upon a time and a half . . ."

• • •

Why do Puerto Ricans even bother to get driver's licenses?

Because they come in handy for cashing bad checks.

• • •

SO
GROSS
EVEN
WE WERE
OFFENDED

• • • • • • •

What is the perfect gift to give a dead baby?

A dead puppy.

• • •

What is the difference between karate and judo?

Karate is a martial art, while judo is what bagels are made from.

• • •

What is the most common pickup line in a lesbian bar?

"Your face, or mine?"

• • •

Why shouldn't we make fun of handicapped people?

If it weren't for them, we wouldn't be able to get great parking spots.

• • •

How do we know that the bottom half of women were designed by Polacks?

Who else would have placed the shithole so close to the snack bar?

• • •

A girl about to be married confessed to her close friend that she was not, as she had promised her fiance, a virgin. She asked her friend what to do.

"No problem," said the friend. "Just buy a piece of raw liver and shove it up inside you. It will make you tight and he will never know the difference."

The girl followed this advice and on her wedding night the horny groom consummated the marriage—in the bed, on the floor, and in the bathtub. The bride fell asleep blissfully, but when she awoke she was devastated to find the following note pinned to her pillow:

"Dear Jane: Last night was pure heaven. Unfortunately, since we will never be able to repeat that performance, I am leaving you forever.

"P.S. Your vagina is in the sink."

• • •

Why do women have faces?

So men can tell the vaginas apart.

• • •

What's the difference between a hog and a man?

A hog doesn't have to sit in a bar and buy drinks all night just so he can fuck some pig.

• • •

Why do black kids have bigger dicks than white kids?

Because white kids get toys to play with.

• • •

What do you say to a feminist with no arms and no legs?

Nice tits, bitch.

• • •

What tastes good on pie but not on pussy?

Crust.

• • •

How can you tell if someone is half Catholic and half Jewish?

When he goes to confession, he takes a lawyer with him.

• • •

What is the definition of a Greek?

A guy who believes in enlarging the circle of his friends.

• • •

Two fags were walking down the street and passed a handsome guy. One fag turned to the other and said, "See that stud there, Bruce?"

"Sure," said the second fag.

"Well, let me tell you, he's a tremendous fuck," the first fag said.

"No shit?" his friend asked.

The first fag replied, "Well, hardly any."

• • •

What's the definition of a "hermaphrodite?"

A bisexual built for two.

• • •

How can you tell if you're in a gay church?

Only half the congregation is kneeling.

• • •

What do you get when you cross Rogaine and Viagra?

Don King.

• • •

Why do women have foreheads?

So you have somewhere else to kiss them after you cum in their mouths.

• • •

What do you call balls on a faggot?

Mudflaps.

• • •

A boy comes to his father and asks, "Dad, what does a vagina look like?"

"Well my son," the father says, "before sex it looks like a perfect pink rosebud with a sweet perfume."

"Well then," asks the kid, "what does it look like after sex?"

His father asks, "Well, son, have you ever seen a bulldog eating mayonnaise?"

• • •

How can you tell when a Jewish American Princess really dislikes sex?

When she even has her guppies fixed.

• • •

Why do Jewish brides always smile at their weddings?

Because they know that they've given their very last blowjob.

• • •

When do Jewish men stop masturbating?

When their wives die.

• • •

Do you know why it's so hard for women to uri-nate in the morning?

Have you ever tried pulling apart a cold cheese-burger?

• • •

What are they going to give Michael Jackson if he molests one more small boy?

His own parish.

• • •

What is black and has twelve green tits?

The garbage bag at a breast cancer clinic.

• • •

What is a Mexican's idea of safe sex?

Locking the car door.

• • •

How do you know when your girlfriend has been taking too many steroids?

When she comes home, yanks your pants down, and fucks you in the ass with her clit.

• • •

Did you hear about the dyslexic who tried to commit suicide?

He threw himself behind an oncoming train.

• • •

Why does Bill Clinton have a hole in his penis?

So he can think with an open mind!

• • •

What's the difference between Princess Di and JonBenet?

One was killed by paparazzi and the other was killed by Papa Ramsey.

• • •

Did you hear about Woody Allen's latest movie?

It's called, *Honey, I Married the Kids.*

• • •

Why does Slick Willie take Hillary with him every-where he goes?

So he won't have to kiss her good-bye.

• • •

What's the new movie about Michael Jackson called?

The Hand that Robs the Cradle.

• • •

THE WORLD'S SHORTEST BOOKS

The Code of Ethics for Lawyers
The Black Guy's Book of Foreplay
Jerry Garcia's Guide to Beating Drug Addiction
Career Opportunities for History Majors
Dr. Kevorkian's Collection of Motivational Speeches
George Foreman's Big Book of Baby Names
Mike Tyson's Guide to Dating Etiquette
The Amish Phone Book
Great Women Drivers Of Today

• • •

What's black and blue and hates sex?

A rape victim.

• • •

So a man answers the telephone, and it's an Emergency Room doctor. The doctor says, "Your wife was in a serious car accident, and I have bad news and good news."

"What's the bad news?" asks her husband.

The doctor says, "The bad news is she has lost all use of both arms and both legs, and will need help eating and going to the bathroom for the rest of her life."

The husband says, "My God. What's the good news?"

The doctor says, "The good news is, I was only kidding. Your wife's dead."

• • •

Why are men so concerned about the size of their penises?

Because they should be.

• • •

What's the definition of disgusting?

Stuffing a dozen oysters into your granny's cunt and sucking out thirteen.

• • •

What's a man's definition of a romantic evening?

Sex.

• • •

How can a girl tell if her date is a real loser?

His teddy bear is equipped with a vagina.

• • •

How did you know that you've had a good blowjob?

When you have to burp her to get your balls back.

• • •

What is the difference between a new wife and a new dog?

After a year, the dog is still excited to see you.

• • •

What has four legs and one arm?

A happy pit bull.

• • •

Where does a redneck go to get takeout food?

Highway 101.

• • •

How does a redneck know when his meat is cooked?

When the tire marks are gone.

• • •

What's the difference between a female lawyer and a pit bull?

Lipstick.

• • •

What's worse than a male chauvinist pig?

A woman that won't do what she's told.

• • •

Why do men want to vote for a female for President?

Because we'd only have to pay her half as much.

• • •

"I'm afraid I have some good news and some bad news," the doctor says to the female patient.

"Well, give me the good news first, Doc," she says.

The doctor replies, "Your lab tests came back today, and your crabs are all gone."

She says, "Gee, that's great! But what's the bad news?"

The doctor tells her, "We don't know what killed them."

• • •

How can a redneck tell if he had a good time at the party last night?

He wakes up in a pool of his own puke.

• • •

How do you insult a flasher?

Tell him you've seen ten-year-old kids hung better than he is.

• • •

Did you hear what the NFL is doing with the next draft?

They are giving the first three picks to the Philadelphia zoo.

• • •

What do you get when you cross a Korean chef and a French poodle?

Dinner.

• • •

What do you get when you have a group of women with PMS and yeast infections?

A whine and cheese convention.

• • •

Why should you always puke in the gutter when you're drunk?

So bums can have breakfast in bed.

• • •

An interviewer asked Stevie Wonder how he felt about being born blind.
"Well, it could have been worse. I could have been born black!"

• • •

A young man was showing off his new sports car to his girlfriend. She was thrilled at the speed. "If I do 200 mph, will you take off your clothes?" he asked.

"Yes!" said his adventurous girlfriend. And as he gets up to 200, she peeled off all her clothes. Unable to keep his eyes on the road, the car skidded onto some gravel and flipped over. The naked girl was thrown clear, but he was jammed beneath the steering wheel.

"Go and get help!" he cried.

"But I can't! I'm naked and my clothes are gone!"

"Take my shoe," he said, "and cover yourself."

Holding the shoe over her pubes, the girl ran down the road and found a service station. Still holding the shoe between her legs, she pleaded to the service station proprietor, "Please help me! My boyfriend's stuck!"

The proprietor looked at the shoe and said, "There's nothing I can do for you . . . he's in too far."

• • •

What did the blind-mute-quadraplegic get for his birthday?

Cancer.

• • •

What's the difference between Virginia and Arkansas?

In Virginia, Moosehead is a beer. In Arkansas it's a misdemeanor.

• • •

What do you call a woman who knows where her husband is every night?

A widow.

• • •

How does a man show that he is planning for the future?

He buys two cases of beer.

• • •

What did the fag do when he found out his boyfriend was a leper?

He shit a dick.

• • •

How do you get a bunch of Mexicans out of your house?

Tell them a Taco Bell truck is overturned on the freeway.

• • •

Did you hear what happened to the guy in the black gin mill who yelled "Fire?"

Everybody did.

• • •

What is the real reason Arab women wear veils?

So they can blow their noses without having to use their hands.

• • •

Why did Lisa Marie and Michael Jackson finally get divorced?

1. She wanted children. So did he.
2. She liked to suck big dicks, he liked to suck little dicks.
3. The night he got rushed to the hospital was the first time she had ever seen him in bed.
4. He was always getting into her makeup.

• • •

How can you spot the Italian woman in a cow pasture?

She's the one without a bell.

• • •

How can you tell that a Polack has wandered into the forest?

All the bears are lighting fires to drive him back out.

• • •

How does a romance novel set in Harlem end?

The hero gets the heroin.

• • •

Why does a Jewish American Princess close her eyes during sex?

So she can pretend she's shopping.

• • •

Did you hear about the new auto insurance policy for Jewish mothers?

It is known as the "My Fault" policy.

• • •

A Puerto Rican, who was new to New York, walks up to a beautiful woman on the street and asks, "Do you know where Central Park is?"
    "No, I don't," she replies.
    "Too bad," the Puerto Rican says. "I guess I'll just have to rape you right here."

• • •

Did you hear about the Polack who got fired from his job of cleaning the toilets in casinos in Las Vegas?

He was skimming off the top.

• • •

Why was Robin Givens always black and blue?

Because Mike Tyson usually knocks before he enters.

• • •

How can you tell if a Polack has been drinking from the toilet?

His breath smells better.

• • •

Did you hear about the guy who finally figured out women?

He died laughing before he could tell anybody else.

• • •

What is the difference between the typical white teenager and typical Puerto Rican teenager?

The white teen wants to make honor roll, and the Puerto Rican wants to make bail.

• • •

Why are there so few black novelists?

Because it usually takes them five to ten years to finish a sentence.

• • •

What's the difference between a lawyer and a trampoline?

You should take your workboots off before you jump on a trampoline.

• • •

Why do women pierce their bellybuttons?

For a good place to hang their air fresheners.

• • •

Why did God give women legs?

So you wouldn't have to drag them into the bathroom and douche them after fucking them.

• • •

How did the father know his daughter was masturbating during her period?

He caught her red-handed.

• • •

What is definitely gross?

While you are fucking some broad, her tapeworm gives you head.

• • •

What do you call a girls' soccer team when they are all having their periods?

The red socks.

• • •

Did you hear about the midget who got fired by his female boss?

He kept getting in her hair.

• • •

GROSS CELEBRITY JOKES

• • • • • • •

Why does the tunnel in Paris get so red?

Because they got Di all over it.

• • •

What's the difference between Princess Di and Tiger Woods?

Tiger got a better driver.

• • •

There's a new organization out there to fight drunk driving . . . .

M.A.D.D., Monarchs Against Drunk Drivers.

• • •

What's the difference between a Mercedes and a Porsche?

Diana wouldn't be seen dead in a Porsche!

• • •

Why is Nancy Reagan miffed at Princess Diana?

Because Diana gets to wear the next Versace collection before she does.

• • •

What do you give the princess who has everything?

A seatbelt and an airbag.

• • •

What's Di getting for Xmas?

The Queen Mother.

• • •

What's the difference between the London Ritz and the Paris Ritz?

You get mints after dinner at the London Ritz and minced after dinner at the Paris Ritz.

• • •

What's the one thing that attracts Diana more than a wealthy Egyptian?

A solidly-built Pole.

• • •

Of course, I could add that the police at the scene didn't need to add chalk outlines. . . .

There was Di all over the road.

• • •

What's the difference between a Mercedes 600 and a can of Spam?

They give you a key to get the meat out of a can of Spam.

• • •

Why was it questionable if Princess Diana would have made a good queen?

She had tunnel vision.

• • •

Why did Elton John sing at Diana's funeral?

The Crash Test Dummies couldn't make it!

• • •

How many paparazzi does it take to kill Di?

50. One to drive in front of Di and 49 to take pictures.

• • •

What does DIANA stand for?

Died In A Nasty Accident.

• • •

What is the difference between Princess Di and Prince William?

One is the heir to the throne and the other was thrown through the air!

• • •

What do a tampon and Princess Diana have in common?

They both go into dark tunnels and come out covered in blood.

• • •

What does DODI stand for?

Died Opposite DI.

• • •

What did Mother Teresa ask Diana the last time they met?

"Can you give me a crash course in media recognition?"

• • •

What did St. Peter say to Dodi when they met at the Pearly Gates?

"Talk about being royally screwed!"

• • •

What did the Pope say when asked, "Why was Diana more popular than Mother Teresa?"

"Well, Di did have a more smashing personality."

• • •

What would Di be doing if she were alive today?

Scratching at the lid of her coffin.

• • •

Why did Elton John take his boyfriend to the funeral?

So at least one old queen would be seen crying in public.

• • •

What do Lady Di and Pink Floyd have in common?

Their last greatest hit was the WALL.

• • •

What did Dodi say to Di before they left the Ritz?

"Do you want to sleep here or crash in the car?"

• • •

What do Diana and George Burns have in common?

They both died when they hit 100.

• • •

What was the last thing to go through Diana's mind?

The dashboard.

• • •

What does Princess Diana have in common with Hugh Grant?

They both bought it in the backseat of a car.

• • •

Did the British Secret Service kill Princess Diana?

No, the French underground did it.

• • •

What's worse than getting red wine off a carpet?

Getting Di off the upholstery.

• • •

DI AND DODI TOP FIVE RECORDS

Leader of the Pack
Lord, Won't You Buy Me A Mercedes-Benz?
Die Like an Egyptian
Dead Man's Curve
How Much is that Dodi in the Window?

• • •

What's the title of the new Princess Diana movie they are making?

One Wedding and a Funeral.

• • •

What does a bee have in common with a Mercedes?

They both make royal jelly.

• • •

How do you spoil Princess Diana?

Leave her out in the sun.

• • •

Did you hear that Princess Diana was suffering from PMS?

Pulverized Mercedes Syndrome.

• • •

What's the difference between Lady Di and the East Germans?

The East Germans survived the wall.

• • •

What's the bumper sticker on Fergie's car?

I brake for paparazzi.

• • •

What's the difference between Chappaquiddick and Junior's crash?

It only took Ted four hours to call the cops this time.

• • •

Where was JFK, Jr. during flight school?

Studying for the bar exam.

• • •

What was JFK, Jr.'s favorite movie?

The Prince of Tides.

• • •

The Coast Guard contacted Ted Kennedy with the news that JFK, Jr.'s body had been located.

"We have good news, better news and great news," they said. "The good news is that we have recovered the body."

"What's the better news?" inquired Ted.

"Well, when we pulled him up, he had several nice-sized lobsters and a dozen blue crabs on him."

Horrified, Ted asks, "What's the great news?"

"We're pulling him up again tomorrow!"

• • •

Have you heard that Mattel is bringing out a JFK, Jr. doll?

Some Assembly Required.

• • •

How did Ted Kennedy teach his children to swim?

First you get out of the car and float to the surface!

• • •

Why won't they cremate uncle Teddy when he dies?

It will take two weeks to put the flames out.

• • •

What did John, Jr. tell his housekeeper before he left?

"You feed the dog. I'll feed the fish."

• • •

What did JFK, Jr. tell his wife and sister-in-law before the flight?

"Bring a bathing suit."

• • •

What's the difference between Elvis and JFK, Jr.?

Elvis was bloated BEFORE he died.

• • •

What's another difference?

They're still looking for Elvis.

• • •

What did St. Peter say to the Grim Reaper?

"For the last time! I said TED KENNEDY! Not Joe, not John, not Robert, not Michael, not Jackie, and not John, Jr! I said TED!"

• • •

They say John F. Kennedy, Jr.'s left wing fell off.

Sounds like a right wing conspiracy.

• • •

What was the forecast for Cape Cod?

Cloudy, with widely scattered bodies and debris.

• • •

What do the Kennedys fear the most?

Old age.

• • •

What was the best thing about JFK, Jr.?

He was just a plane down-to-earth guy.

• • •

What was the temperature off of Martha's Vineyard after JFK, Jr's plane went down?

Three below.

• • •

What does JFK, Jr. miss most about Martha's Vineyard?

The runway.

• • •

Did you hear that Kennedy Airport in New York is being renamed?

They're calling it Kennedy & Son.

• • •

Hear about Air Alaska's new route?

It flies from JFK to JFK, Jr.

• • •

Why is the Coast Guard like a horny fourteen-year-old boy?

They both get excited about finding a wet, crumpled *Playboy.*

• • •

What was JFK, Jr.'s last wish?

He wished he'd had more air time.

• • •

What do JFK, Jr. and Rock Hudson have in common?

They both died off of Gay Head!

• • •

Why was John-John flying that night?

Ted offered him a lift.

• • •

What could have been JFK, Jr.'s last words?

"Sex and flying don't mix when you are the pilot."

"I dropped my cigarette—it didn't roll over toward the gas cap, did it?"

"Shit, we almost hit that duck!"

"Ya' know, we really should visit the family cemetery this year."

"If you had wings, dear, you'd be an angel."

"Do you remember the last time we met Princess Di?"

"Carolyn, your sister gives a much better blowjob than you do."

• • •

So Jeffrey Dahmer has his parents over for dinner. His mom kept bitching at him, saying, "I hate all your friends."

Jeffrey says to her, "So just eat the salad."

• • •

How did Jeffrey Dahmer like to spend his spare time?

He had friends over for lunch.

• • •

What were Dahmer's last words to the guy that killed him in the fight?

"Hey buddy, I used to eat guys like you for breakfast!"

• • •

Did you hear about the new Jeffrey Dahmer freezer?

Seats six and more headroom.

• • •

What was Jeffrey Dahmer's favorite drink?

An Old Milwaukee with no head.

• • •

Did you hear that Jeffrey Dahmer's old apartment is up for rent?

It's a three bedroom, partially furnished, room-mates included, some assembly required.

• • •

What did Jeffrey Dahmer do if he didn't like his neighbors?

He scraped them off his plate.

• • •

Why did Jeffrey Dahmer hate eating vegetables?

There was no room in the closet for the wheel-chairs.

• • •

What did Jeffrey Dahmer have in his refrigerator?

About ten pounds of ground Chuck.

• • •

What did Jeff say to O.J. in jail?

You show me yours, I'll show you theirs.

• • •

What's the difference between Jeffrey Dahmer and O.J. Simpson?

Dahmer used a FORK and a knife.

• • •

What's Jeffrey Dahmer's favorite meal?

Frank and beans.

• • •

Why did Jeffrey Dahmer keep a blender on his porch?

He liked to greet his guests with a warm hand-shake.

• • •

How did David Koresh find out he was Jesus Christ?

God spoke to him through a burning building.

• • •

How many Branch Davidians can you fit into a phone booth?

All of them . . . in the coin slot.

• • •

Why did Koresh have so many wives?

They made excellent matches.

• • •

What does WACO stand for?

We Ain't Coming Out
White Anglo Cook Out
We Are Crispy Outside
We're A Combustible Organization
We Are Crispy Outlaws

• • •

What was David Koresh's new holy day?

Ash Monday.

• • •

What does it say on David Koresh's tombstone?

Roast in Peace.

• • •

What does KFC stand for in Waco?

Koresh's Fried Christians.

• • •

What do you call O.J., David Koresh, and Jeffrey Dahmer in a jail cell together?

A well balanced breakfast: Juice, toast, and serial.

• • •

NOW THAT'S SICK!!

● ● ● ● ● ● ●

Why do women have periods?

Because they deserve them.

• • •

A third grade teacher in the Bronx decided to see if city kids knew what sounds farm animals made. She asked the kids to put their hands up if they knew the correct sounds.

"Who knows what sound a cow makes?" she asked.

Mary put her hand up and said, "Mooooo!"

"Very good," replied the teacher. "What sound do sheep make?"

"Baaaa," answered Billy.

She continued this for a while. Then she asked, "What sound does a pig make?"

All the hands in the class went up. She was surprised at the response. She chose Little Tyrone at the back of the class. He stood up, took a deep breath, and screamed, "Up against the wall, mutha-fucka!"

• • •

A cucumber, a pickle, and a penis were comparing relative woes one day. The cucumber said, "I have it really bad. I am allowed to grow big and fat. But then they pick me, drown me, slice me into little pieces, and finally eat me. It's all over then."

"Well," said the pickle, "at least your suffering is brief. Mine is prolonged. Like you, I am allowed to grow big and fat. But then I am picked and bathed in foul smelling fluid for what seems an eternity, and then they eat me, too."

"So what?" answered the penis. "At least there is an end to it for you two. My torture is daily and eternal. I also am allowed to grow big and fat. But then they always wrap a rubber bag over my head, put me in a dark, wet cave that smells like fish, and make me do pushups until I puke."

• • •

What are the only three occasions on which an Italian sees a priest?

At his baptism, at his marriage, and before his electrocution.

• • •

Now That's Sick!!

Ten-year-old Stevie had been blind since birth. One night his mother came into his bedroom before he went to sleep and told him that he must pray very, very hard because tomorrow was a special day and he would get a wonderful surprise. So Stevie fell asleep praying with confidence that he would be able to see the next day.

His mother awoke Stevie early and told him to open his eyes, as this was that special day she had promised him. Stevie tried, but then cried out, "Mommie, Mommie, I still can't see!"

"I know, dear," she said. "Today is April Fool's."

• • •

Why are there two X's on bottles of Dos Equis beer?

Every Mexican needs a co-signer.

• • •

How can a teenager tell if a case of acne is really bad?

A blind man tries to read his face.

• • •

What is the most common pickup line used by black guys?

"Scream, bitch, and I'll kill you."

• • •

A sheriff in Alabama drove up to the scene of a freshly reported major accident, where he found a local farmer filling in a large trench. "What y'all doing, son?" he asked.

"Well, sheriff," he replied, "I am just doing the right thing. This busload of blacks just got plowed into pieces by the passing train. Killed 'em all. I'm just given 'em a decent burial."

"Whoa, son, that was fast," the sheriff said. "Y'all sure every one of 'em was dead?"

"Well, two or three of 'em kept sayin' they weren't, but you know how them black folks lie all the time."

• • •

What is the hardest part about changing your sex from a man to a woman?

Sewing in the anchovies.

• • •

So this gay guy was brushing his teeth and flossing in front of the bathroom mirror, when he noticed that his gums had started bleeding.

"Thank God!" he exclaimed. "Safe for another month!"

• • •

Did you hear why the black guy had a heart attack on Halloween night?

Someone came to his door dressed as a job.

• • •

Why don't women have brains?

Because they don't have penises to carry them around in.

• • •

What do you get when you cross a Jew with a black?

A kid who feels guilty about being on welfare.

• • •

How can you tell if the Arkansas wedding is formal?

The shotgun is painted white.

• • •

How can you tell you're in a feminist bookstore?

There is no humor section.

• • •

What do Hillary Clinton and J. Edgar Hoover have in common?

They're both female impersonators.

• • •

Two Polacks met and one asked the other why he appeared so depressed.

"Because I just got back from taking my dog to obedience school," the first Polack says.

"Didn't your dog pass the course?" the second one asks.

"Sure," the first Polack says, "but he learned to sit up and roll over three days faster than I did."

• • •

How can you tell if an Italian girl is old-fashioned?

She has a handlebar moustache.

• • •

What is the busiest day at a Harlem whorehouse?

Father and daughter night.

• • •

How is an Italian hearse different from a regular one?

In an Italian hearse, the body is always in the trunk.

• • •

What is another name for homos with AIDS?

Tool and die workers.

• • •

A boy was making his confession to his priest.

"I have this problem with spontaneous erection since I turned thirteen," the boy confesses. "I know it is a sin to play with myself. Can you help me?"

"I think I can lick your problem for you," the priest says.

• • •

What do you call a Jew wearing a gas mask?

A poor sport.

• • •

What was the last thing that went through Kurt Cobain's mind when he shot himself?

The roof of his mouth.

• • •

What are the three reasons that make anal sex better than vaginal sex?

It's warmer, it's tighter, and it's degrading to women.

• • •

What are the two signs your kid is being molested at his day care center?

He won't stop crying unless you put a pacifier in his asshole, and you have to play strip poker with him to get him into the bathtub.

• • •

How many Italians does it take to change a lightbulb?

Four. One to steal it, one to change it, one to keep lookout, and one to shoot any witnesses.

• • •

What do you say to a blonde with no arms and no legs?

"Nice tits!"

• • •

What's the difference between sushi and pussy?

Rice.

• • •

How can you tell if you're a loser?

Your girlfriend wants to have sex in the backseat of your car and insists that you drive.

• • •

What is the difference between a blonde and a brunette?

A brunette is looking for Mr. Right. A blonde is looking for Mr. Right Now.

• • •

Hear about the mortician who was also a necrophiliac?

He just loved to bury himself in his work.

• • •

Now That's Sick!!

Hear about the new computer viruses?

CLINTON VIRUS
Gives you a 7 inch hard drive with no memory.

VIAGRA VIRUS
Makes a new hard drive out of an old floppy.

LEWINSKY VIRUS
Sucks all the memory out of your computer, then emails everyone about what it did.

LORENA BOBBIT VIRUS
Re-formats your hard drive into a 3.5 inch floppy, then discards it through Windows.

RONALD REAGAN VIRUS
Saves your data, but forgets where it is stored.

MIKE TYSON VIRUS
Quits after two bytes.

OPRAH WINFREY VIRUS
Your 300 MB hard drive suddenly shrinks to 100 MB, then slowly expands to 200 MB.

ELLEN DEGENERES VIRUS
Disks can no longer be inserted.

• • •

What is the most effective way to scare off a black mugger?

Threaten to wipe a booger on his new tennis shoes.

• • •

What does a girl with bulimia call two fingers?

Dessert.

• • •

What's grosser than having your girlfriend pass you her gum while you French kiss her?

When she tells you it wasn't gum.

• • •

One night, Bill Clinton is so worried about the Federal budget crisis that he can't get to sleep. So he gets up and goes for a jog in the moonlight. As he passes the Lincoln Memorial, he wonders, "What would Honest Abe have done in this situation?"

So he kneels down in front of Lincoln's statue and says, "Oh Lincoln, Lincoln, I want to do what's best for the country, but I don't know what that is."

And sure enough, Clinton hears a disembodied voice coming from within the monument, saying, "Go to the theater."

• • •

What is the cruelest gift you can give a queer epileptic?

A vibrator.

• • •

What is the cruelest gift you can give Helen Keller?

A paint-by-numbers set.

• • •

What is the kindest gift you can give a deaf person?

A Yoko Ono album.

• • •

What did one faggot say to the other faggot at the gay bar?

"Can I push your stool in?"

• • •

A guy runs into an ex-girlfriend, with whom he didn't have the greatest relationship.

He says to her, "You know, I was with another woman last night, but I was still thinking of you."

"Why, because you miss me?" his ex asks.

"No," he replies. "Because it keeps me from coming too fast."

• • •

Now That's Sick!!

Did you hear about the new brand of tires— Firestein?

They not only stop on a dime, they pick it up.

• • •

An artist asked the gallery owner if there had been any interest in his paintings, which were on display.

"I have good news and bad news," the owner replied.

"What's the good news?" the artist asked.

"The good news is that a gentleman inquired about your work and wondered if it would appreciate in value after your death," the gallery owner said. "When I told him it would, he bought all fifteen of your paintings."

"That's great," the artist exclaimed. "What's the bad news?"

The gallery owner replied, "The guy was your doctor."

• • •

A farmer was sitting in the neighborhood bar getting hammered. A man came in and asked the farmer, "Hey, why are you sitting here on this beautiful day, getting drunk?"

The farmer shook his head and replied, "Some things you just can't explain."

"So what happened that's so horrible?" the man asked as he sat down next to the farmer.

"Well," the farmer said, "today I was sitting by my cow, milking her. Just as I got the bucket 'bout full, she lifted her left leg and kicked over the bucket."

"Okay," said the man, "but that's not so bad."

"Some things you just can't explain," the farmer replied.

"So what happened then?" the man asked.

The farmer said, "I took her left leg and tied it to the post on the left."

"And then?"

"Well, I sat back down and continued to milk her. Just as I got the bucket 'bout full, she took her right leg and kicked over the bucket."

The man said, "Again?"

The farmer replied, "Some things you just can't explain."

"So, what did you do then?" the man asked.

"I took her right leg this time and tied it to the post on the right. Then I sat back down and began milking her again. Just as I got the bucket 'bout full, the stupid cow knocked over the bucket with her tail."

"Hmmm . . ." the man said and nodded his head.

"Some things you just can't explain," the farmer said.

"So, what did you do?" the man asked.

"Well," the farmer said, "I didn't have any more rope, so I took off my belt and tied her tail to the rafter. In that moment, my pants fell down and my wife walked in . . .

"Some things you just can't explain."

• • •

WHAT ARE THE FIVE STANDARD PENIS SIZES?

1. Is it in yet?
2. Small
3. Medium
4. Large
5. Nice. Just where do you think you're going to put THAT?

• • •

So a little boy and girl are taking a bath together.

The girl looks between the boy's legs and said, "What's that? Can I touch it?"

The little boy said, "Of course not, you already tore yours off."

• • •

A gay guy hears that one of his boyfriends was in the hospital, so he goes to visit him. His friend looked terrible, so he asked him what all had happened.

"Well, they cut out my tonsils, pulled out all of my teeth, and removed my hemorrhoids."

"You don't say!" the gay guy exclaims. "A total hysterectomy!"

• • •

Why did the Clintons have only one child?

Because Hillary had a vasectomy.

• • •

Did you hear about the town nymphomaniac?

She was so skinny that every time she swallowed an olive, five guys skipped town.

• • •

What is a woman doing while looking at a blank sheet of paper?

Reading her rights.

• • •

How do you know when you are getting old?

When you start having dry dreams and wet farts.

• • •

How can you tell if your little boy will grow up to be homosexual?

He likes to play Lick the Can.

• • •

Why do black people like fingerbowls in restaurants?

So they can wash the silverware before they steal it.

• • •

What do men and pantyhose have in common?

They either cling, run, or don't fit right in the crotch.

• • •

Why is a man like a lawn mower?

If women aren't pushing one around, then they're riding him.

• • •

Now That's Sick!!

How do Ethiopians get circumcised?

Butt fuck their sisters and let the tapeworm do the job.

● ● ●

Do you know the difference between a Catholic wife and a Jewish wife?

The Catholic wife tells her husband to buy Viagra.
The Jewish wife tells her husband to buy Pfizer.

● ● ●

Give a man a fish and he will eat for a day.

Teach him how to fish and he will sit in a boat and drink beer all day.

● ● ●

Why can't Hanson masturbate?

With all that blonde hair it's hard to find their pussies.

• • •

What is grosser than gross?

When you sit on Santa's lap and he pops a boner.

• • •

What is grosser than that?

When he stands up and you don't fall off.

• • •

TOP 11 REASONS TO GO TO WORK NAKED

1. Your boss is always yelling, "I want to see your ass in here by 8:00!"
2. Can take advantage of computer monitor radiation to work on your tan.
3. Inventive way to finally meet that hunk in Human Resources.
4. "I'd love to chip in, but I left my wallet in my pants."
5. To stop those creepy guys in marketing from looking down your blouse.
6. You want to see if it's like the dream.
7. So that—with a little help from Muzak—you can add "Exotic Dancer" to your resume.
8. People stop stealing your pens after they've seen where you keep them.
9. Diverts attention from the fact that you also came to work drunk.
10. Gives "bad hair day" a whole new meaning.
11. No one steals your chair.

● ● ●